Passion for photography and love for Jamaica bring together an idea of the unique photo book about Jamaica. If you are asking yourself "why visit Jamaica?" Jamaica has a proud and astounding culture, embracing the land and the lifestyles they lead. Visiting the island is a great time to take an adventurous history lesson.

Katerina Budinova

JAMAICA
THE LAND WE LOVE

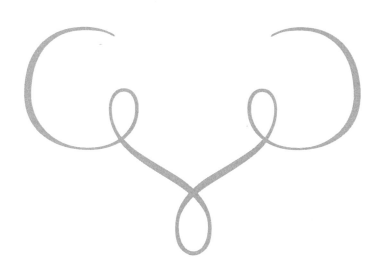

AUSTIN MACAULEY PUBLISHERS™
LONDON • CAMBRIDGE • NEW YORK • SHARJAH

A CIP catalogue record for this title is available from the British Library.

ISBN 9781528977074 (Paperback)
ISBN 9781528977067 (Hardback)
ISBN 9781398414365 (ePub e-book)

www.austinmacauley.com

First Published (2020)
Austin Macauley Publishers Ltd
25 Canada Square
Canary Wharf
London
E14 5LQ

Special thank you to Michal, Neisha and Puchi without them this book will never be made. Thank you from the bottom of my heart for your commitment. You are not only a valued member of this group, you're a dear friend. I can't imagine working without you.

Special thank you to all people of Jamaica and their help with this photobook.

Very special thank you to:

Michal Šott

Stacy-Ann Dawkins

Noel Dawson

Photographer of this stunning book
Michal Šott giving all the respect to
local Dan Dawson's family.

All honour to
one and every one,
who cooperated and never give up.

Katerina giving all the respect
to everyone involved in this project
specially to her brother Michal.

Special thanks to
Austin Macauley Publishers

Katerina Budinova - Author
Michal Šott - Photographer

Sister & Brother

"One Love"

Jamaica: The Land We Love

Photography Book will introduce Nature, Culture & Local People.
You will be taken to sunny beaches, inside city life and day to day lives of local people.
You are going to meet those, who make up today's Jamaica.
We will visit a place where the most famous Jamaican Bob Marley lived.
We are honoured to introduce pride of Jamaican's people on annual march of Maroon's in Accompong Town.
You will see amazing life of Jamaican's farmers & fisherman's.
You will see how to cook authentic Jamaican food and also life of Rastafari movement or local musicians.
You will see secret hidden places, known only by the locals.
Tropical nature, fruits, flowers and rainforests.
Birds, lizards & crocodiles.
Photography book Jamaica: The Land We Love also introduce life in the ghetto and some of the most dangerous places on Island.
From South to North, from East to West of the island and adventures of the country life.
The book introduce tourists well known localities,
where millions of tourists coming every year
to spend their life time holidays.

JAMAICAN'S FISHERMEN

DUNN'S RIVERS FALLS

23

BLACK RIVER

NEGRIL BEACH

KINGSTON

KINGSTON
TRENCH TOWN

Trench Town violence continues

Vincient 'Tarta' Ford

No Woman, No Cry
Bob Marley and the Wailers

In appreciation to

THE PEOPLE OF THE
FEDERAL REPUBLIC OF GERMANY

For the renovation of this museum wing of
The Trench Town Culture Yard

THE COMMUNITY OF TRENCH TOWN
OCTOBER 8, 2003

DANIEL POWER TRENCH
1813 - 1884

FRANCES CHARLOTTE MACKAY

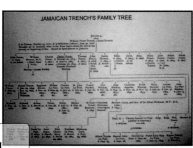

JAMAICAN TRENCH'S FAMILY TREE

TRENCH TOWN
kingston 12   jamaica

The Government Yards of Trench Town

FLAT BRIDGE

BIRD CENTRE

COLUMBUS PARK

COFFEE PULPER
ACCOFFEE PULPER FORMERLY USED IN
ST DACRE AREA TO EXTRACT COFFEE
BEAN PRIOR TO DRYING

BELL FROM THE LAST STEAM LOCOMOTIVE
USED BY THE JAMAICA RAILWAY
CORPORATION
PRESENTED TO DON C. TRETZEL
CHAIRMAN, BOARD OF DIRECTORS
1960 - 1974

CANOE

JAMAICA DI 1494

COLUMBUS PARK 1968
THIS PARK WAS DEVELOPED BY THE KAISER
BAUXITE COMPANY. IT IS MAINTAINED AS A
SCENIC ATTRACTION AND REPOSITORY FOR
ITEMS OF HISTORICAL INTEREST.

MONTEGO BAY

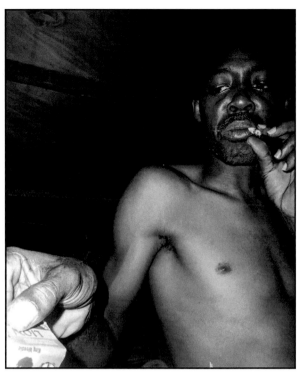

OCHO RIOS

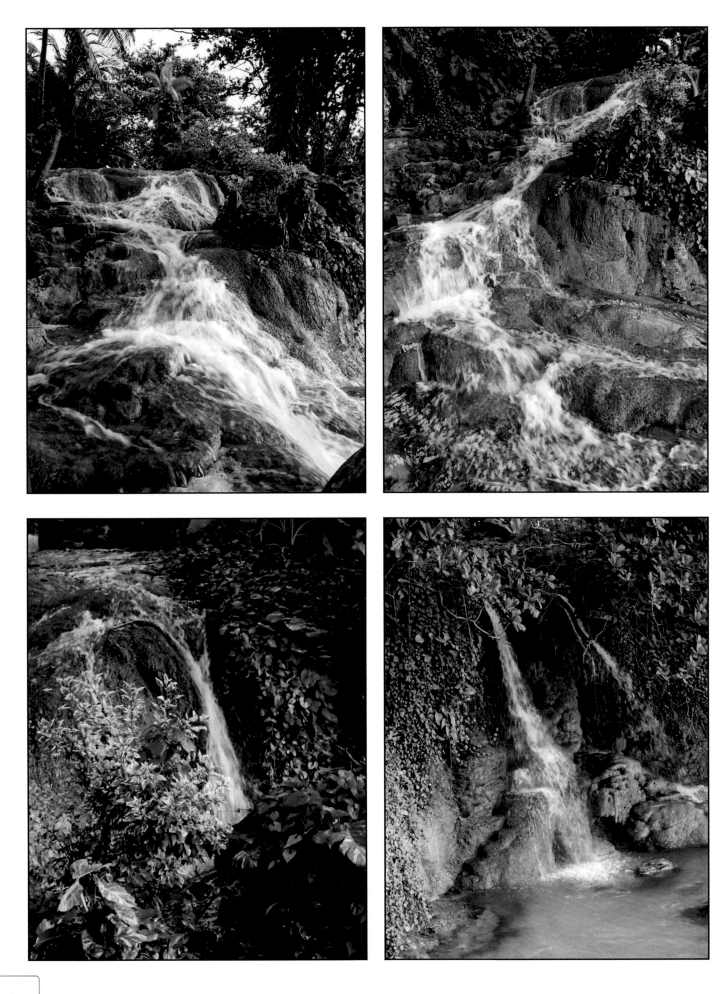

FALMOUTH

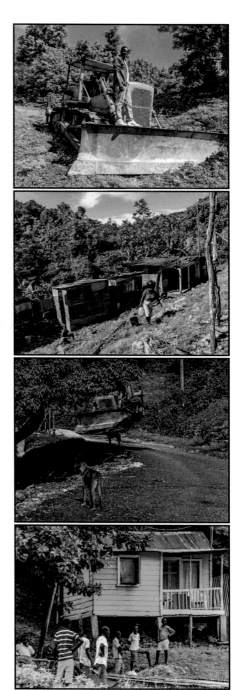

FIRE WATER

117

BLUE LAGUNE

WAKEFIELD

124

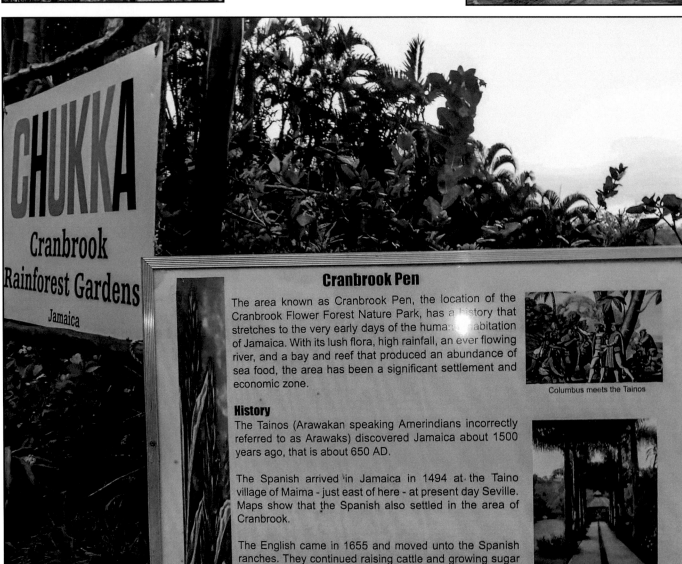

Cranbrook Pen

The area known as Cranbrook Pen, the location of the Cranbrook Flower Forest Nature Park, has a history that stretches to the very early days of the human habitation of Jamaica. With its lush flora, high rainfall, an ever flowing river, and a bay and reef that produced an abundance of sea food, the area has been a significant settlement and economic zone.

Columbus meets the Tainos

History

The Tainos (Arawakan speaking Amerindians incorrectly referred to as Arawaks) discovered Jamaica about 1500 years ago, that is about 650 AD.

The Spanish arrived in Jamaica in 1494 at the Taino village of Maima - just east of here - at present day Seville. Maps show that the Spanish also settled in the area of Cranbrook.

The English came in 1655 and moved unto the Spanish ranches. They continued raising cattle and growing sugar cane. The earliest English map showing Cranbrook dates to 1839. Cranbrook is here identified as a pen or a cattle ranch and is listed together with the Bellevue estate.

Cranbrook Flower Forest

130

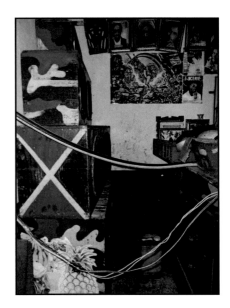

JAMES BOND BEACH

135

SAVANA - LA MAR

141

143

156

WESTMORELAND

ZOO

GOOD HOPE

JOHN CROO

175

LIZARDS

SAINT ANN PRIORY BEACH

184

185

SANT ANNE NINE MILE

213

BOG WALK

231

PORT MARIA

245

ST JAMES FARMERS

251

253

YS FALLS

OPENING HOURS: 9:30 a.m. - 3:30 p.m.
CLOSED ON MONDAYS
AND ALL PUBLIC HOLIDAYS
GROUP LIMIT IS 25 PERSONS (Max)

ENJOY YOUR VISIT WITH NATURE

BLUE MOUNTAINS

PORTLAND LOWER ST. ANDREW. UPPE

285

FAITH PEN

ST. MARY PARISH, CALABASH FISHERMAN

MONTPELIER, ANCHOVY, PAPAYA FARM

298

JOHNS HALL
ADVENTURE
TOURS

PRODUCT OF JAMAICA

ACKEE AND SALTFISH

APPLETON ESTATE RUM TOUR

GREAT RIVER

GOLDEN SPRING

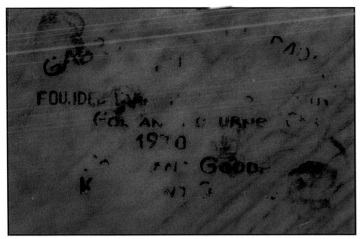

LIBERTY HALL

DOCTOR'S CAVE BEACH MONTEGO BAY

NATHANEL DAWIS
KNOWN AS "NATY"

SELASSIE I SAYS

"FROM TRUTH ALONE IS BORN LIBERTY AND ONLY AN EDUCATED PEOPLE CAN CONSIDER ITSELF AS REALLY FREE AND MASTER OF ITS FATE. IT IS ONLY AN EDUCATED PEOPLE THAT REPRESENTATIVE AND DEMOCRATIC ORGANS OF GOVERNMENT CAN EXERCISE THEIR INFLU--ENCE FOR NATION PROGRESS."

CTION TO THE WORDS

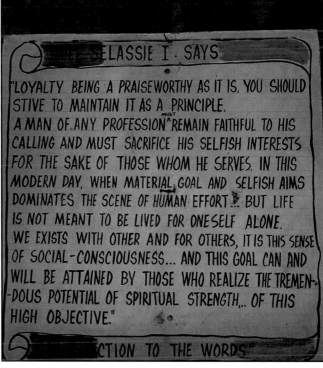

SELASSIE I. SAYS

"LOYALTY BEING A PRAISEWORTHY AS IT IS, YOU SHOULD STIVE TO MAINTAIN IT AS A PRINCIPLE. A MAN OF ANY PROFESSION MUST REMAIN FAITHFUL TO HIS CALLING AND MUST SACRIFICE HIS SELFISH INTERESTS FOR THE SAKE OF THOSE WHOM HE SERVES. IN THIS MODERN DAY, WHEN MATERIAL GOAL AND SELFISH AIMS DOMINATES THE SCENE OF HUMAN EFFORT... BUT LIFE IS NOT MEANT TO BE LIVED FOR ONESELF ALONE. WE EXISTS WITH OTHER AND FOR OTHERS, IT IS THIS SENSE OF SOCIAL-CONSCIOUSNESS... AND THIS GOAL CAN AND WILL BE ATTAINED BY THOSE WHO REALIZE THE TREMEN--DOUS POTENTIAL OF SPIRITUAL STRENGTH... OF THIS HIGH OBJECTIVE."

CTION TO THE WORDS

SELASSIE I SAYS

"BRACE YOURSELF FOR HARD WORK AND POOL YOUR RESOURCES TO COMPETE WITH OTHERS IN ECONOMIC AND COMMERCIAL ACTIVITIES OF YOUR MOTHERLAND. ... LET US BE CONSCIOUS OF OUR RESPONSIBILITES AND FIRMLY DISCHARGE OUR OBLIGATIONS THEREBY BECOMING MASTERS OF OUR DESTINY.
"IT IS BETTER TO TILL THE LAND THAN TO BICKER ON TRIVIAL MATTERS."
"DO NOT FALL PREY TO IDLENESS FOR IT SHALL BE A CURSE TO YOU AND TO SUCCEEDING GENERATIONS. YOU MUST SET YOURSELF UP AS AN EXAMPLE OF DETERMINATION & HARD WORK"

ACTION TO THE WORDS

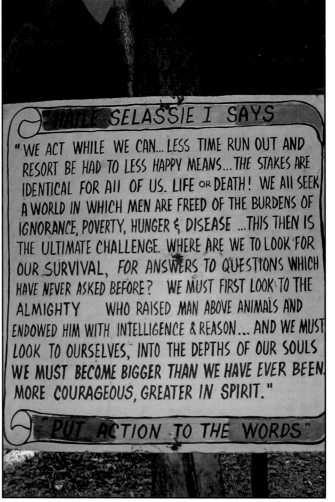

HAILE SELASSIE I SAYS

"WE ACT WHILE WE CAN... LESS TIME RUN OUT AND RESORT BE HAD TO LESS HAPPY MEANS... THE STAKES ARE IDENTICAL FOR All OF US. LIFE OR DEATH! WE All SEEK A WORLD IN WHICH MEN ARE FREED OF THE BURDENS OF IGNORANCE, POVERTY, HUNGER & DISEASE ...THIS THEN IS THE ULTIMATE CHALLENGE. WHERE ARE WE TO LOOK FOR OUR SURVIVAL, FOR ANSWERS TO QUESTIONS WHICH HAVE NEVER ASKED BEFORE? WE MUST FIRST LOOK TO THE ALMIGHTY WHO RAISED MAN ABOVE ANIMALS AND ENDOWED HIM WITH INTELLIGENCE & REASON... AND WE MUST LOOK TO OURSELVES, INTO THE DEPTHS OF OUR SOULS WE MUST BECOME BIGGER THAN WE HAVE EVER BEEN. MORE COURAGEOUS, GREATER IN SPIRIT."

"PUT ACTION TO THE WORDS"

THE ACCOMPONG TOWN - Maroons

FLANKERS

SACRED TO THE MEMORY
OF
JACQUELINE GORDON
OCT. 4, 1971
MARVETTE HOFFSTEAD
NOV. 11, 1970
MICHELLE JARRETT
JUNE 3, 1970
SOPHIA JOHNSON
MAY 28, 1973
DEON MURRAY
SEPT. 2, 1971
CASSANDRA LEWIS
JULY 6, 1970
ADOLPHUS ROSE
MARCH 10, 1969.

WHO DIED TRAGICALLY
ON FRIDAY MARCH 22, 1985.

*I THANK MY GOD UPON EVERY
REMEMBRANCE OF YOU.*
PHILIPPIANS 1:3.